The Clergy Conversations

Dealing Practically with the Person Behind The Pulpit

Dr. Robert O'Keefe Hassell

Foreword By: Bishop Anthony W. Gilyard

ROYSTON
Publishing

BK Royston Publishing
P. O. Box 4321
Jeffersonville, IN 47131
502-802-5385
http://www.bkroystonpublishing.com
bkroystonpublishing@gmail.com

© Copyright – 2018

All Rights Reserved. No part of this book may be reproduced, stored in a retrieval system, or transmitted by any means without the written permission of the author.

Cover Design: Cameron Wallace, www.thewallaceproject.com

ISBN-13: 978-1-946111-67-8

Printed in the United States of America

A Letter To Others Just Like Me…..

Never in a million years would I have thought I would have been a minister of the gospel or in active ministry leadership. Frankly, I had life all planned out. So much for the plan, huh? Nevertheless, I can agree with the following sentiments, once stated by one of my former first ladies who is now resting in the arms of the Lord, "When you come to the end of yourself, you come to the beginning of God." With God, truly, this has bas been one of the most challenging journeys of my life. It has carried, even in its most difficult moments, a reward of overcoming daunting feats and becoming holistically great by God's design.

Accepting and embracing God's call, mandate, and commission for my life was a life-changing series of experiences. I wish I could tell you that everything happened over night. However, it did not at all. The process continues to be rigorous, regimented and refining to say the least. However, the most critical lessons in my personal ministry have been how to live a balanced life, learning to discover who I am both naturally and spiritually while in process, and work diligently to effectively function in the call to which I have been commissioned.

In this book, you will discover areas of concern that have the tendency to be overlooked and ignored among ministry leaders of all classifications. These issues are paramount to both ministerial and personal development. This book is not another "self-help or how to" book, but an honest sentiment to express the importance of maintaining the vessel and the anointing in your life. As you go forward in your natural life and ministry, remember that God has the authority and authorship concerning your outcome. Be encouraged. Be steadfast. Remain confident. As the Bible states in *Philippians 1:6 (KJV)* – *"Being confident of this very thing, that he which hath begun a good work in you will perform it until the day of Jesus Christ."*

Pursue with Promise,

Dr. Robert O'Keefe Hassell

Dedication

This book is dedicated to five great generals of the faith who have been essential to my development and formation as a Minister of the Gospel. They have all served in the role of fathers and mothers in specific areas of my life to teach lessons that are essential to both the man and the minister.

Reverend Earl Dirkson – Pastor Emeritus of the Trinity Missionary Baptist Church (Cookeville, Tennessee). You are not just my father in the ministry, but you are a solid example of the posture of selflessness that is required to serve the people of God. You have given freely of yourself over the years to the ministry, the church and your family. Because of your ministry, people have come to know Christ in so many ways. I am the preacher and ministry leader I am today because of your willingness to invest the most treasured parts of yourself into my ministry and me as a person. I am your living time capsule. From the days of picking me up on the side of the road for church in rain, shine, sleet or snow to simply being a fixture of unwavering faith in my life, you have never failed to be there. You are my Elijah – I am because you are.

The Late Elder A.Z. Hall – Former General Secretary of the Church of God in Christ (COGIC) and Pastor of Pentecostal Assembly COGIC (Jackson, Tennessee). You recognized the hand of God on my life in its earliest stages. You protected me and made impressions on my personal ministry that will last a lifetime. You instilled within me the epitome of a "true" servant's heart. You helped me to see God in the impossible places through the eyes of faith.

Pastor Breonus Mitchell, Sr. – Pastor of the Mt. Gilead Missionary Baptist Church (Nashville, TN). I appreciate you for placing full confidence in me to work, learn and share under your tutelage at the former Greater Grace Temple Community Church (Nashville, Tennessee). Who would have known showing up to church early one Sunday would have placed me in the direct presence and in servitude to one of the greatest ministry gifts this side of heaven? Serving you and your congregation in leadership taught me the weighty responsibilities of carrying a congregation in heart and leading them unconditionally through life's unpredictable circumstances. It was through you I learned what "God's grace" looks like in real life.

Overseer Teddy Jackson (Dad) – I appreciate you for being the fixture of "restoration." I went through a period when I thought I lost it and was hopeless on so many levels. You never let me forget who I was and you walked me each step until I gained my confidence back. You restored me and helped me rediscover all that God had purposed for me. You were the reactivator! Your prayers of recovery, resurrection and revival saved my life. Dad, you were my "Pastor" in the truest sense. You helped me navigate through my humanity and usher me into the face of an authentic freedom I never knew before. I am grateful you took the time to understand and listen. You challenged me to produce even in pain. You let me cry, you let me process, but you pushed me to be productive even in pain. You continue to give me wisdom, push me to destiny and to pursue God with everything I have in me. Thank you for ushering me back into the presence of "wholeness" again. I love you Overseer!

Table of Contents

A Letter To Others Just Like Yourself	iii
Dedication	v
Foreword	xi
Review	xiii
Chapter 1	1
"I Didn't Ask For This!	
Chapter 2	19
"Hooping, But Hopeless!"	
Chapter 3	31
"The Breaking Point."	
Chapter 4	49
"When Revelation Meets Reality"	
Chapter 5	61
"From Grace to Growth!"	
References	75
About The Author	77

Foreword

Are we called on the basis of need? You cannot be the person in the pulpit only because you want to meet a need, but you must be there because God sent you. We do not come into ministry, but God sends us. How can they hear without a preacher and how can they preach expect they be sent? No matter your experience in ministry, age or classification in ministry, this read will give you hope.

The Conversations that will be discussed will not be just about the call, but about the person. You cannot allow anything or anyone, including you, to cause you to deviate from the set pace and the place of God's will for your life. Many hang the total success of their ministry assignment on the level of the anointing. They do so without taking time to maintain a healthy and whole vessel mentally, spiritually and physically.

As you read, be prepared to have what I will call the 5A's of this conversation; *Awareness* of your humanity, *Acceptance* of your mission, *Alignment* of the right places and people, *Anointing* to see results and *Acceleration* for the ordained speed to accomplish. The lack of authenticity is due to the lack of being in touch with our humanity. The attire will not prove anything whether it is a high regalia of ecclesiastical garments or "jeans and timbs" to be relevant to the audience, clothes cannot cover you.

Genuine growth will happen when you embrace your place of vulnerability and not be fixated on your strength. Public figures have now become private fixtures in the minds of clergy who have lifted people from the pulpit and now have them on pedestals, but just as greatness can be seen, so can weakness.

"We are dismantled by the things we refuse to deal with!"
-Dr. Robert O' Keefe Hassell

Allow this read to help you revisit, redefine and recommit to your borders and your balance.

Bishop Anthony W. Gilyard
Founding Pastor of Bethlehem Judah Christian Fellowship
Elizabeth, NJ
www.bjcfinc.org

Review

The Clergy Conversations: Dealing Practically with the Person Behind The Pulpit is necessary read for individuals who are currently in or have been recently appointed to leadership capacities within ministry. Additionally, the book is full of insight and clarification for lay members as well. I urge everyone to read this book, and apply it to their life. It will change your life!

Dr. Robert O'Keefe Hassell perfectly describes the rises and falls, challenges and triumphs, purpose and destiny of being one who is called to lead and teach God's people. The role of a leader, in any capacity, is difficult because of the example you must set. You must become the standard in order for those you are leading to want to hear, listen to, and follow that which you teach. This book deals with the struggles we face, how to overcome them, and how to develop the ability to teach others to do the same without giving up or going insane.

As explained, most people called and chosen to do ministry did not ask to be. There are very specific ways to except the call, and walk it out with grace and excellence. Dr. Hassell very profoundly breaks these down.

Dr. Hassell states, "It was not that I had a problem with the call. I had an issue with God over the interruption of my life, the weight of expectation, the scrutiny of being young and in ministry, handling the processing of my anointing, and the feeling of being on exhibit like a zoo animal." As a 24 year old Pastor, I can whole heartedly relate to this statement. Though I have been in ministry in one capacity or another since I was 9 years old, I still had to endure the same hardships as any other young person going through school. Peer pressure, judgmental eyes, ridicule for not being like everybody else, and to add to all that I had the weight of church responsibility. I did not hang out like everyone else, do the things everyone else did, or even have the desire to do so. Dr. Hassell clarifies that "The call is personal, but extends beyond the locality of who we are. It requires our commitment, dedication, perseverance and sacrifice." I sacrificed what my peers thought I should be or do in order to answer 'The Call.' The only way this was and continues to be possible is with the grace of God. I have developed a good relationship with Him, which allows me to hear revelation and apply it. As a result, I take those things and teach those I lead how to do the same.

There are days I want to give up or throw in the towel because of the weight of the anointing, but I do not. The writer of the hymn "Solid Rock" pens, "My hope is built on nothing less than Jesus' blood and righteousness." Dr. Hassell affirms that, "Hope is the resting place where we can reside when life happens. Our anchor holds us during places of turbulence and inconsistency. Hope is what keeps us focused amid unusual circumstances." No truer words have been spoken! Hope and faith are important to being the best person behind the pulpit we can be.

The Clergy Conversations: Dealing Practically with the Person Behind The Pulpit will also help lay members of the church. It will allow them to see and understand what it truly means to be a leader in ministry. I believe it gives an inside, behind the scenes look at the life and heart of both men and women in ministry. Many church members feel that life for us is easy because of the call, that we do not endure anything, know anything about life, or feel what they feel when we have to go through life. This is especially true if you are a young pastor like myself who pastors members that are old enough to be my parents or grandparents. Dr. Hassell is a living breathing perfect example of how false those beliefs are.

Being chosen by God is an honor and a privilege, but it does not mean that it is a light thing to carry. Nor does being called by God have to mean that you are miserable and have to carry the weight alone. This book has encouraged me in so many ways. I believe it will encourage anyone who is already in leadership, about to begin his or her journey in ministry and leadership, or follows a leader that is called of God regardless of your age.

Overseer George R. Logan III, *Senior Pastor & Founder*
Cathedral of Deliverance Ministries Inc.
Pittsburgh, Pennsylvania

Clergy

/ˈklərjē/ *noun*

Noun: **clergy**; plural noun: **clergies**

The body of all people ordained for religious duties, especially in the Christian Church.

Chapter 1
"I Didn't Ask For This!"

"The difference between being CALLED and CHOSEN is SOVEREIGN SELECTION. Either way, you do not have a CHOICE in that DECISION."

-Dr. Robert O'Keefe Hassell

Many of us who God has called spend years coming to grips with what God has called us to do. The majority of the time what he has called us to do totally has a way of hijacking our initial plans for our own lives. God's call totally interrupts and sometimes alters everything that we had imagined ourselves becoming in life. Truthfully, I never wanted to be a minister, preacher or anything of the sort. However, I always say that God snuck me per se. I resisted tooth and nail. I fought the entire way. I did not kick and scream, but I rebelled and ran in my own unique way. Many of us that are called into the ministry have difficulty adjusting and embracing the process because we never seem to "fit." As much as we make attempts to be normal and live a regular life, nothing is ever ordinary. Our walk with God becomes unique and pushes us into places we have never imagined we would go.

I was saved at the age of the seven, under the Pastorate of Rev. Alvis Thurman at the New Fairview Missionary Baptist Church in Rome, Tennessee. Unlike many others, I was adamant about "making it in" at a very young age. Salvation was the requirement, but heaven was the goal. As a gift one Christmas, I received a Star Search microphone and some old choir robes. I would be in my room preaching to my toys. I would hold real life revivals in my room. I would preach, shout, and falling out from dusk until dawn. Looking back, I get a kick out of my mom. My mom would come in and say, "Give the benediction! Cause church is over." She was tired of my "joyful noise." Most people would consider it play, but something about it was real to me. People could always see that! I believed God could do anything and I wanted everybody to know that too. I believe those moments were the essential beginnings that foreshadowed who I would become in the future. There was always a conviction and urge to bring everybody I possibly could with me. Make no mistake about it, I love God. I love His Church. Most importantly, I love his people. As a young adolescent, those things never left me.

THE CLERGY CONVERSATIONS

Fast-forward to my college years, I was your typical person. Rose up in the social ranks, popular, extremely active in student activities, in a fraternity and I felt as if I was invincible. I was a "church boy" as they called me in College. My frat gave me a secular presence, but I never quite escaped the "church boy" label. Sunday mornings, people would be out on the yard early playing cards, smoking, checking each other, and enjoying Sunday doing absolutely nothing. Here I come with my Bible in hand, headed to meet the church van. It was such a dreadful walk. Hearing taunts like, "Look at the little church boy!" "Going to church again, for what?" "Bro, look at him!" The craziest thing was, when those same people got in crisis or needed sound counsel; I was the first one they called. I cannot even begin to tell you how many people I had to pray for that I did not like. I cringed at the thought of helping a known enemy, especially the ones that made life difficult for me on the regular. Proverbs 25:21-22 (KJV) says, *"If thine enemy be hungry, give him bread to eat; and if he be thirsty, give him water to drink: For thou shalt heap coals of fire upon his head, and the LORD shall reward thee."* I was not thinking about a reward. Let us not forget Luke 6:27-36. I said to myself, "God, your people are mean and pretentious. If this is what pastors and ministry leaders deal with on the regular, you can change my assignment to something else." Little did I know, I was shepherding people and really did not know it.

At this juncture of my life, I met a man by the name of Elder A.Z. Hall. He was the Pastor of the Pentecostal Assembly Church of God In Christ (COGIC) in Jackson, TN and the General Secretary of the Church Of God In Christ. Elder Hall recognized that God's hand was on me. He made every stride and effort to remind me that God had a plan for my life. He understood that I was odd, quirky yet cool, prophetic, articulate, highly analytical, opinionated upon observation and changing fast. He saw my charisma and influence on people. He saw my leadership and ability. He understood my humanity. He was, without a doubt, one of the greatest pastors I ever had.

One Sunday, at 'The Assembly' 452 N Hays Ave - Jackson, Tennessee 38301, church was too live! All the Saints were in rare form, on fire and "seeing everything." Church was like that all of the time! It was in that moment, Elder Hall called me up and prophesied to me. Unbeknownst to me at the time, he would literally prophesy my life from that moment in 2005 to present. I will never forget it. Time seemingly stood still, I felt like I was the only one in the room and it was if God was informing me of my future, no matter if I was ready to accept it or not. I can hear his voice clearly that day saying the following:

"Robert O'Keefe Hassell, as much as you might try, you will never fit!"

"God will place you for a purpose that is predicated on his will and not what you have planned!"

"In order to be sanctified, you must learn embrace being set-apart and separated from what you desire to settle in!"

"You are intelligent, quick-witted and analytical – Nevertheless, God must free you from the bondage of your own mind so that your potential manifest and you come to know the godly wisdom that is required to sustain it.

"You have a peculiar anointing that God will not allow to be placed in the wrong hands. Your life is attached to it!"

The last statement he made was "You will walk alone, but you will not be by yourself! God understands what you feel, so it is okay to cry. However, His will for your life will not change. Walking in the will of God is never easy, but God will grant you a specific, intentional grace for every level of anointing you will be given."

It was at this point that my entire life entered a paradigm shift. Everything started to move fast. The word had been given. I thought I had more time. In all honesty, I did not. I graduated in April of 2007. Fresh out of college, there comes these speaking engagements. Pastor Jeffrey Huddleston calls my phone and says, "Son, I want you to come speak for our Youth Day service. I have already contacted your Pastor and he has said you can come." I was a ball of nerves because I tried to repeatedly rationalize what I knew was happening. At this point, that is where the running from God began. I went on did the Youth Day Service. It was one heck of a service. My uncle Pastor Earl Dirkson talked to me forever after the fact and said, "Son, it won't be long now. Your time is coming!" Invitations to speak kept coming in and I was going everywhere. However, life changed for me the summer of 2011. Pastor Raymond Burns, Senior Pastor of the Baird's Grove Missionary Baptist Church, called my phone. I was thinking to myself, "Okay, another Youth Day! I can prepare a little motivational message and be out of there as quick as I came in!" However, that was not what he asked me. He said, "O'Keefe we want you to come and do our Youth Revival." I was like, "Pastor Burns, I am not a preacher. There are some other people out there you could choose from other than me." He said, "I have talked to Pastor Dirkson and expressed that you are a voice that the young people need to hear in this hour. I will see you on these dates." It was my very first 3-Day revival. I called my uncle in shock. He responded, "You will be fine." The church was packed all 3 nights. It was on the Friday night of the revival that I had an encounter with God. I ran into him while I was on the run. After preaching and working an altar packed with young people seeking God, I went out like a light. What seemed like seconds was like the longest series of moments. It was supernatural and literally beyond words. I woke up in the arms of the 1st Lady of the church with my mother at my side. I open my eyes and came back to consciousness. . I knew from that moment forward that I had been marked with a distinction and a destiny, one that I could not escape.

I heard the voice of God once again during the summer of 2011, but I was reluctant to fully embrace the calling on my life. I had a "Moses Experience," as referenced in Exodus 4:10, where I pleaded with God and offered up excuses. I thought they were good ones. Besides, I figured there were enough pastors, preachers and leaders in the world. Why could I not be one of the normal ones? What made me an exception? After all, God could find someone else right? However, God did not let me off the hook that easy. God used me at every opportunity while making evident "the call and assignment" that was on my life. I was on the road frequently traveling to numerous churches in the Tennessee-Area and abroad, working with various Youth groups as well as speaking at Conferences and Revivals under Pastoral supervision and guidance. Yet, at the end of it all, I was still in denial. It was not that I had a problem with the call. I had an issue with God over the interruption of my life, the weight of expectation, the scrutiny of being young and in ministry, handling the processing of my anointing, and the feeling of being on exhibit like zoo animal. I already stuck out like a sore thumb. I had become used to being different. I found a way to make my difference "cool." I frankly, felt that the preaching and the ministry style that was being birthed in me took away all of my cool points. In my mind, being a preacher eliminated all of the fun. Nevertheless, I found myself submitting.

I announced my calling to ministry on Sunday, October 27, 2013 at Trinity Missionary Baptist Church in Cookeville, Tennessee. I was licensed to preach the gospel on Sunday, November 24, 2013 at the Trinity Missionary Baptist Church under the leadership of Reverend Earl Dirkson. On December 9, 2017, I was ordained as an Elder in the Churches of God In Christ, Inc. (COGIC) - Tennessee

Eastern 2nd Jurisdiction by Bishop James M. Scott. Now, I am here today! It is not a journey I regret either. I will say there are times when we never see the fullness of ourselves because we are so focused on our limitations. More often than not, the very the thing that we desire to be is "limited." Matter of fact, it is too limited for the place that we were designed for in the context of our destiny.

The acceptance of the call from God is a place of divine decision for many of us. Decisions are a "crossroads" that God initiates through interruption and intervention. These defining moments in our lives are where we choose which paths to take in order to reach a certain destination. Orchestrated intentionally by God, our decision to choose God comes with a subsequent series of saying "yes" when we really want to say "no." What we must understand is that our decision to choose God and his call are relative. They are subject to our desire and free will, which make them so detrimental to the outcome of our destiny. Over the years, especially in the context of ministry, my relationship with God has continued to evolve and deepen in ways that I have never imagined. I had moments when I wanted to go the other way and even ignore the subtlest promptings. However, just like the loving Father God is, he gives you time to come around and then he speaks.

As I approach these new chapters of my life as both a man and minister of the Gospel, God has placed me in certain situations where I have had to yield and make a "destiny decision." A "destiny decision" is a choice that relates directly to your purpose, which propels you to your assignment that leads to your destiny (which is the fulfillment of your purpose). In these simple conversational moments with the Creator, he broke things down to me in the most profound way.

Urgency vs. Complacency

The call of God is a carrier of destiny. Destiny cannot wait! Therefore, we have to move with a sense of urgency. We do not have as much time as you think. Whether we want to face it or not, we do not have as much time as you think. The world keeps moving and time is swiftly passing. We will not be young forever! Nor does time stop and wait on any of us to figure it all out. Complacency has no place on the road to destiny. What we have to realize is that each moment that we have is one that we must convert into something great! We must fill each minute of our lives and inject it with purposeful intent in conjunction with the will of the father that is pushing us toward the next level. We cannot seek the acquisition of material things or positions, but set our efforts towards a greater understanding of our God-ordained destiny and the fulfillment God's agenda working through us while in this earth. Complacency is the hesitancy or reluctance to move towards completing an initiative Complacency makes the way for us to become content. Contentment prompts us to enter into a state of stagnancy. As a result, our personal and spiritual growth comes to a halt. The call of God attaches itself to the development of our destiny. Destiny does not allow you to drag your feet.

Priority vs. Play-Time

We have all been guilty of "playing." We play with stuff in a child-like manner, not taking seriously the priorities that are essential. We all have played and I will admit there were times that I played a little too much. Thankfully, God has a way of putting us in check and making us realize the value of choosing priority over playing. 1 Corinthians 13:11 (KJV) says, *"When I was a child, I spake as a child, I understood as a child, I thought as a child: but when I became a man, I put away childish things."* There comes a time when you have to make your priorities a priority God is a God of order and not chaos. When we make the effort to engage the call of God head on, we do so with the understanding that the fulfillment of the mandate and our progress towards destiny depend on tackling the priorities of God's agenda. God's agenda is to "grow us" into the persons, we were intended to be since the beginning of time. This requires us to take inventory of our lives in truth. We have to initiate the hard task of eliminating those conditional people, unhealthy relationships, toxic connections, bad habits and unnecessary involvements. God is challenging us to clean our lives of the clutter and get our priorities straight. We cannot fulfill and make destiny decisions regarding the call of God with clarity by playing around in a bunch of randomness. God challenged me to examine at my life at a variety of angles. As a result, I saw how much time I was wasting and how much I was losing pouring small pieces of myself into unnecessary distractions that kept me busy just for the sake of it. When I was able to eliminate the unnecessary, I was able to pick up the necessary tools that I needed to get me to the next level.

As humans, created by God, he has gifted each us with many abilities and attributes. One of those things being free will. We have many conscious choices to make in this life. However, our choices affect both the natural and the spiritual outcomes that manifest in our lives. When we make the choice of choosing our own agenda, we wind up getting into trouble. Frequently, it is trouble we do not even anticipate or expect. We feel that our way is the best way. When in fact, it is the wrong way! The fact that we choose to do it our way puts us in situations that result in a series of experiences where we are forced to learn lessons the hard way! When you choose God's call and intentionally accept his perfect will for your life, you always win. It is not guaranteed the road will be easy or the most comfortable. In spite of this, you will be safe and secure because you are in the safest place you could possibly be. God has plans for you! He desires you give you an expected end according to Jeremiah 29:11. Why not entrust your life to someone who already knows the end before the beginning? God has every single detail under his control. Guess what? You have to be absolutely okay with that. Choose the call! Pursue your destiny! Isaiah 55:8 (KJV)-*"For my thoughts are not your thoughts, neither are your ways my ways, saith the LORD. For as the heavens are higher than the earth, so are my ways higher than your ways, and my thoughts than your thoughts."*

Any day that we choose to live and walk under the weight of this calling requires us to handle things in different ways. Ministry is full of surprises, as we all know. It comes with a great deal of handling the unexpected. Many of us are not ready when God chooses to call us for whatever reason.

We can offer up a myriad of excuses, make suggestions of people whom we know are more qualified, and that actually want it. However, on the contrary, God is always on the search for the "unlikely, unconventional, and unqualified." He seemingly perfects purpose in the most unexpected areas within the lives of people. Becoming a minister or working any leadership capacity within ministry automatically puts your life under the microscope. Everything that you are is now up for public viewing. At this particular place, you must understand that there are several things that await you on this path. Observation and criticism will meet you at every angle. In most cases, there will be days when you feel as if your life is not your own. The truth behind that statement is that it is not. Frequently, we tell God on the regular, "I didn't ask for this!" The honest sentiments regarding this reality is that we did not at all. We were sovereignly selected for a purpose much bigger than we planned for and a destiny that extends beyond what we comprehend.

In most cases, the conditional logistics of our lives did not match the call. We were not wayward or doing any and everything. It was just that preaching and ministry were some of the farthest things from our minds. Many of us had plans for life. Although they were "good plans," they were not "God's plans." Therein, I have discovered, lies the difference. We have to understand, no matter where we are in ministry, that God's calling on our lives carries inconvenience that seemingly conflict and alter our life plans. Honestly, I never planned to be a minister of the Gospel or work in ministry leadership. I was satisfied with being the typical Christian man. I wanted to make good money, be respected in my community, be highly educated, have a nice home, teach Sunday school, be the "favorite" Deacon that everyone loved and that gave all the kids candy. It was my goal to be "that man," but never the one that had to stand behind that pulpit. Too much spotlight, a whole lot of sacrifice, politics, having to be nice 24/7, bridling your tongue, midnight and early morning calls. It was not my ideal choice. I had seen my uncle Pastor for 25+ years and grew up in the Church. I was there every time the doors opened. I was with the Pastors, Preachers and the Deacons. The Deacon Board was seemingly the place to be!

However, as I have begun this lifetime journey with God, I understand the significance of two things. These two factors assist me in reconciling who I am, the role I play in the agenda of the Kingdom and my responsibility as an ambassador of the Gospel. Two critical factors are alignment and anointing. When it comes to alignment, God does some of his most progressive yet proactive work by establishing a nature of conviction. In our conviction, there is a call to action that moves us into a state of doing the tasks that are assigned to us. What we must come to understand is that alignment precedes the assignment. There is no way we can complete or engage the assignment when we are not in the correct posture or position to embrace it. The alignment serves as a catalyst or propellant to push us into the place of preparation. Alignment for God's purposes are often unconventional. Alignment is a process that is defined by a series of experiences that are good, bad or indifferent. These experiences put us in positions where we are challenged to exhibit great faith, see the impossible and simply trust beyond what we understand. More often than not, the details are absent. Nevertheless, these experiences assist us in shaping our character and strategically placing the necessary pieces that are priority when it comes down to our functionality in ministry. The Bible says in Zechariah 4:10 (NLT) – *"Do not despise these small beginnings, for the Lord rejoices to see the work begin, to see the plumb line in Zerubbabel's hand."* The beginnings of God's greatest work in regards to your call are the experiences you will encounter on your way to clarity in purpose. Your alignment is a part of the formative process where God takes the hands-on approach by using what is around you to shape you. Our call is defined and refined through alignment. It is at this place where we come to know, in truth, what does not fit and why. The call, itself, remains a mystery and is revealed by God through Gods free course in using our lives to reach beyond ourselves. The call is personal, but extends beyond the locality of who we are. It requires our commitment, dedication, perseverance and sacrifice. It requires us to relinquish "our plan" to pick up "his plan."

Secondly, there is the anointing. The anointing is not only the endorsement or validator for the work, but it serves as the foundation that pushes us to zeal and fervor in carrying out the work of the ministry in any capacity. The anointing allows our calling to truly be sustained by warranting our dependence and reliance to be totally on Christ. The privilege of being called and anointed is a great responsibility. The anointing and its operation is a reminder of how deeply we all are in need of God. The anointing of God keeps us. For it is by the Spirit that we are taught and that we learn everything that we need to know to execute our divine assignment. Through alignment and anointing, God creates a set pace and synchronicity on every level. By entering into a regimented process, the pursuit of God echoes the intent for our lives and to become the manifested vision that rooted in purpose. Our acceptance of that calling means that we say yes to God and fearlessly abandon anything that does not work toward his ends as well as his will. We can answer the call of God with confidence in knowing that God does not leave anything uncultivated in the life of the vessel. He uses every strength, weakness, heartache, success, relationship, and experience to condition our hearts for the journey. He desires that we draw us closer to him, so that he can prepare us to fulfill our life's calling. God created us for his work, agenda, purpose and pleasure. He has already prepared the work for us to do and will glorify himself through the work of our hands.

Chapter 2

"Hooping, But Hopeless!"

"Do not be fooled by the CLIMATIC nature of a CLOSE. In all actuality, it may be a CRY for HELP. While you are busy SHOUTING in the pews, more often than not, SUFFERING awaits the person behind the pulpit after service."

-Dr. Robert O'Keefe Hassell

We live in a world where there is a looming influence of unbelief, shadows of doubt and tons of questions. So much occurs in the lives of people that we lead in various capacities on a daily basis. Even on our best day, it may cause a reflexive "flinch" within our spirits because it is unexpected and even more complex than we can actually wrap our minds around. As ministry leaders, we are called to minister to the diversities of situations that require and unwavering hope even in the midst of experiencing this whirlwind called life. Hope is essential to our call and commission because it is the catalyst that fuels how we inspire and influence people that we lead. In any capacity, we shepherd them to aspire for greater in the future. Hope is the "good thing" in the future that we desire. Our hope is linked to our expectation, which is a carrier of faith.

It is the very essence of hope that carries the spirit and posture of expectation to receive, which is why we can never lose it. It is our hope that is a desire for something valuable in the future, the thing in the future that we long for, and the foundation or purpose for thinking that our yearning may indeed be satisfied. The Bible says in Job 11:18-19 (KJV) - *"And thou shalt be secure, because there is hope; yea, thou shalt dig about thee, and thou shalt take thy rest in safety. Also thou shalt lie down, and none shall make thee afraid; yea, many shall make suit unto thee."* Hope is the resting place where we can take refuge when life happens. Our anchor holds us during places of turbulence and inconsistency. Hope is what keeps us focused amid unusual circumstances. As ministry leaders, we must maintain a hope within hope. As we lead people to see a God bigger than their present circumstances, we must embody the same hope reflected in Mark 9:23 (KJV) – *"Jesus said unto him, If thou canst believe, all things are possible to him that believeth."* We not only preach, teach, sing, and prophesy with hope; It is a place that must become a habitation of permanent residence. Hope is the resting place of accomplishing and achieving the impossible. Luke 18:27 (KJV) says, – *"And he said, the things which are impossible with men are possible with God."*

In the African-American preaching tradition, there is a celebratory moment that comes at the end of the sermon. It is a juncture where excitement, passion, and energy emphasize with intensity the nature of the call to action. In charismatic church environments, the "close" reignites hope and an optimistic outcome even amid the struggle of attempting to view some of life's most difficult experiences through the eyes of faith. Nevertheless, no matter the emotional response to this climatic moment, sometimes the messenger is the one that is suffering the most. Yes, they are preaching the bright side. However, they are living the dark side. It is difficult to hold on to a hope that seems out of grasp when your difficulty with handling the circumstances of life contradict the very principles of faith you just delivered to give people hope.

Statistics from the *New York Times* (2010) stated the following factors that prove to be alarming:

- ❖ "Members of the clergy now suffer from obesity, hypertension and depression at rates higher than most Americans. In the last decade, their use of antidepressants has risen, while their life expectancy has fallen. Many would change jobs if they could."

- ❖ 13% of active pastors are divorced.
- ❖ 23% have been fired or pressured to resign at least once in their careers.
- ❖ 25% do not know where to turn when they have a family or personal conflict or issue.
- ❖ 33% felt burned out within their first five years of ministry.
- ❖ 33% say that being in ministry is an outright hazard to their family.
- ❖ 45% of pastors say that they've experienced depression or burnout to the extent that they needed to take a leave of absence from ministry.
- ❖ 50% feel unable to meet the needs of the job.
- ❖ 52% of pastors say they and their spouses believe that being in pastoral ministry is hazardous to their family's well-being and health.
- ❖ 57% would leave the pastorate if they had somewhere else to go or some other vocation they could do.
- ❖ 70% do not have any close friends.

- ❖ 75% report severe stress causing anguish, worry, bewilderment, anger, depression, fear, and alienation.
- ❖ 80% of pastors say they have insufficient time with their spouse.
- ❖ 80% believe that pastoral ministry affects their families negatively.
- ❖ 90% feel unqualified or poorly prepared for ministry.
- ❖ 90% work more than 50 hours a week.
- ❖ 94% feel under pressure to have a perfect family.
- ❖ 1,500 pastors leave their ministries each month due to burnout, conflict, or moral failure.
- ❖ Doctors, lawyers and clergy have the most problems with drug abuse, alcoholism and suicide.

As you can see ministry leaders, both men and women, deal with "real life" issues. Sunday morning is simply one day of the week. We cannot desensitize ourselves to the fact that there are situations that not only challenge our faith, but also dim our hope. Our call is attached to our purpose. Many of us, as ministry leaders, have ongoing challenges and struggles. We want to "appear" as if everything is okay. However, life has a way of challenging our faith at the core. Our hopes, dreams and plans seem to fade away in the face of challenging times. Life has a way of presenting places that look impossible in both our ministry and personal lives. Because we have places of struggle, it is often easier to make feeble attempts to hide them than actually deal with them. We find ourselves overcompensating in our singing, preaching and teaching. No matter how successful we may actually be, the person will eventually fall prey to self-sabotage because there is a sense of hopelessness that comes along with the acceptance of these issues as the norm. These issues are abnormal and the can taint us if we are not careful. This hopelessness causes us to succumb and place susceptibilities in the hands of adversaries that are lying in wait to see us fall.

We struggle with depression, criticism, conflict, family problems, sexual problems, stress, burnout, financial problems, and time management. Most ministry leaders are intensely engaged and task driven. They have an unfailing love for the work and the calling on their life. Most of us enjoy most of what we do in ministry. A great percentage of us, all factors considered, would not change our role if we could. We are one with what we do. The way we deliver a sermon does not eliminate the obvious fact that we deal with serious problems that are in demand of an **immediate** solution. A good hoop or close does not take away the fears, anger, anxieties, bitterness, or issues that we feel on the inside. The honest reality is that even after a celebratory in our preaching and ministry leadership, many of us leave that moment to walk straight into feelings of hopelessness and defeat. The experiences of life outside of ministry often overwhelm us. We carry the burdens of the people, their concerns and their issues. By the time we get to ourselves, we have minimal positivity or hope to encourage ourselves in the areas of our life that demand great faith.

The Bible says in 3 John 1:2 (KJV) – *"Beloved, I wish above all things that thou mayest prosper and be in health, even as thy soul prospereth."* We have to be our "best" for ourselves! A holistically healthy leader is able to embody the true essence of hope that we preach, teach and sing so fervently about on a regular basis. We need professional help, assistance and support to process. We need people to encourage and keep us accountable. Help is available. Hope is available. We must simply remove the mask, be honest with ourselves and be authentic in seeking the help that we desperately need to regain our hope and health. The Bible says in Proverbs 13:12 (KJV) – *"Hope deferred maketh the heart sick: but when the desire cometh, it is a tree of life."* Many of us have hopes not only for ministry, but we have hopes for our personal lives. In the face of our present places of impending struggles, it is easy to perceive that we will never get there. Adversity, obstacle and obstruction have a way of making life look rather cloudy. It can even make the simplest dreams or goals seem to be unattainable. It can cause us to self-isolate, become unstable and even inaccessible on a variety of levels. However, we must use faith to push us beyond and into the places that are deemed impossible. We must shed light in the places of our own darkness. We must treat our wounds, bandage them, let our healing begin and walk the path to recovery in God.

Langston Hughes stated in his poem *Dreams,*

> Hold fast to dreams,
> For if dreams die,
> Life is a broken-winged bird,
> That cannot fly.

> Hold fast to dreams,
> For when dreams go
> Life is a barren field
> Frozen with snow.

The times will come when we are called to a place of unexpected suffering or encounter a season of hard trial. We must never forget that we are human. We, as ministry leaders, are not exempt from trouble or struggles just because we are the "called" of God. It is not an easy task to rejoice in these factors even though we understand that they serve a purpose in our growth as representatives for God in the earth. We have to understand that these challenges that confront us test our confidence in the "living hope." They are a series of redemptive works that are necessary for both our perfection and completion. These tests are ones where we are fashioned into the image of Christ, which is the highest form of processing. We must acknowledge that times where doubt or hopelessness desires to creep in that we must seek God with a relentless intensity. There are times that the depth of our faith and spiritual maturity will be tested is when all we have is our reliance on the savior during periods in life that are not so pleasant and when boldly confronting the issues that lie within our own selves. We are never hopeless. We just have to learn to turn our dependency to the one who can assist us in the management of our humanity and the handling of the roles in ministry to which we have been assigned.

In this dispensation of grace, we are called to be leaders but we must possess a relentless hope to stir a generation of diverse people who are not easily convinced of the necessity of relationship with Christ or association with the institution of the church in general. We are up against the notions that people have lost faith in the institution of the church and subsequently lost faith in God because it was the only picture that had been placed before them. It is our job to show them the hope beyond the experience of Sunday morning. It is our sacred task to shine the light of hope into the darkness of the world's unbelief. We must show practical examples of how to infuse hope into the tapestry of life, especially in the places that do not quite make sense. We must use hope as the bridge to bring people, even ourselves, back to God. Hebrews 10:22 (KJV) says, *"Let us draw near with a true heart in full assurance of faith, having our hearts sprinkled from an evil conscience, and our bodies washed with pure water."* As minister of the Gospel in any capacity, it is critical that we never lose our hope. Hope is the catalyst behind our faith. Hebrews 11:1 (KJV) says, *"Now faith is the substance of things hoped for, the evidence of things not seen."* It is our hope that is connected to our faith even in the face of our own struggles. It is our faith that is attached to our vision. Vision is divine and can only be seen and manifested accurately when we extend our faith to see through the eyes of God. When we persevere in hope, anything though appearing to be impossible can actually happen! We must remember that we must have full dependency on the presence of God.

Chapter 3
"The Breaking Point."

"Behind every PREACHER there is a PERSON."

-Dr. Robert O'Keefe Hassell

If we take a look across pulpits, ministerial rosters and leadership, we will find piles of shattered people. We are broken into many pieces. Within all the movement that our positions require, we make strained attempts to put together the pieces that would make us appear to seem functional in the public eye. God sees that we are on the edge of breakdown. God sees our ever-declining state, but we refuse to ask for assistance from the helper. Our pride places us in denial and puts us in a most vulnerable place. We live by the false pretense of "Fake it until you make it!" However, we are simply faking it, failing at it and falling through the cracks.

On Sunday morning, across the nation, churches are filled to capacity with people. There are people who have come to worship. There are people who have come to spectate. There are people who have come to be critical. Whatever the reason, they all are fixated on one period of service, which becomes the focal point of the experience. The message, the man, and the motivation become the highlighted priority of the day. As vessels used by the Most High, we are taught how to handle many things. However, we have failed in the instruction of how to handle our humanity and process hurt coupled with pain in a healthy way. We dance over it. We speak in tongues over it. We sing over it. We teach over it. We even preach over it. We lead over it! However, we never find the courage to confront it!

The waiting congregation does not care what happened to you the evening before. They do not care if you are tired. It does not even matter if you got the dreaded 12 midnight or 3 a.m. call concerning trouble with a member. They are ignorant of the fact that you may be sick or having trouble processing through difficult situations of your own. They are awaiting a Word from the Lord! So, what do you do? You get up and be a Super-Hero. We become the equivalent of Super-Man. We take-off the Clark Kent of everyday life and trade it for a red cape and tights (i.e. – A Bible, Collar and a Cassock/Clergy Jacket). We set off to go save souls and defeat the devil. Sounds so easy, but it is not. We are so busy fighting the devil and preaching the word that we neglect the defeated state of our own person. As apostles, prophets, evangelists, pastors and teachers we must remember that God grants the necessary anointing to carry out the weight and function of our assignments. However, we are very much real people. We have to handle our humanity with attentiveness and self-care. We do ourselves a severe disservice when we maintain the mindset that we are invincible. Our humanity is connected to the authenticity of our experiences, which allows us to connect with people on the many levels that we do.

"Handle The Hurt, So It Doesn't Handle You!"

-Dr. Robert O'Keefe Hassell

It is so easy to become engulfed by everything set before us that we never face up to the hurt that has us in so many feeble positions. In addition to this, we often do not take the time to process how we are positioned. We neglect the places of our own inner hurt. Our hurt is what holds us hostage and we can never exit its grip. We become ineffective and reach a place of burn out in regular life. As a result, our ministry suffers. Many men and women are at the place of giving up on ministry by the moment because it has all become so overwhelming. If we manage to escape the grasp of hurt, many of us are still deal with subsequent traumas. These traumatic feelings attach themselves to the source where it originated. These traumas paralyze and prevent us from accessing purpose so that we can reach destiny. The honest sentiments of every human being would be to avoid places of hurt altogether. Albeit that is rather impossible. Hurt serves a purpose, but how we handle it can cause us to grow or remain in a dysfunctional state. In your life, you will be hurt so many times. Conversely, how you handle that hurt will determine how you will be able to move forward. We not only deal with hurt for the sake of the process to healing, but so we can know true deliverance. The end goal is for us to become mobile, malleable, accessible and teachable.

In ministry, you will come up against places and people that hurt you. Some hurts you will not be able to articulate. There are other places of hurt that you will not even expect to come your way at all. The consistent pattern within churches and our roles as leaders is that we become familiar with hurt. We become so familiar that it creates a looming fear. We become adamant about our safety and we do not want to be hurt again. As a result, we pull away from people creating barriers that keep us from getting out and keep them from coming close to us. We have the tendency to become overprotective, extremely defensive and distant. We disqualify people and continue to push them away for all kinds of reasons. What happens to people who give in to the hurt and hold on to it? What happens to the people who do not know how to let the hurt go? No one can access us. We live out our days burying suppressed hurt, shame, guilt, unresolved issues and are unable to process. It is these issues when left unsettled lead to depression, suicide, drug use, and unhealthy practices that can be detrimental to our ministries.

If we are to be a more effective leaders and shepherds of God's people, we must understand hurt. We must remain close to the people. The exactness of this space is that, by engaging people, we take the risk on being hurt. Sheep will bite! There is a great chance that we may experience the disregard of our feelings, left uncovered or exposed, and even wounded. It is a part of our journey, but it is not the final destination. However, hurt is a risk that is worth taking. Jesus did and still does the same for us. We must embrace the same in the handling of the people, processing through our own hurt and moving forward in faith. We are the people's direct example in how to embrace it, deal with it and move forward from it in peace.

Because we have become public figures and fixtures of the faith movement, it is easy for ministers to live their lives under the expectations of others. We can spend our entire lives building things around people and platforms that we think will matter. At the end of the day, we can take none of these things with us. We live in such a superficial world. It is so easy to be trapped by what we see in front of us. The paradox lies in the fact that it all of what we see takes a lifetime to gain, but can take seconds to lose! We get preoccupied in trying to be somebody else for the gratification of other people. We forget to ask the question: Who does God want me to be? We make plans for our lives, often times with selfish motives, but rarely do we ask ourselves the critical question: What are God's plans for me? We must be willing to listen! We must realize that God will give us the desires of our heart. He will make us the success we strive to be. However, he will not give us anything that will be to our detriment. He wants our character and integrity to go before us in all things. He is the source of all good things. Instead of being anxious, over-zealous or micromanaging a situation, just listen. Many of us would be actually surprised at what God has to say! Keep in mind, whatever he says, it is for your good! Psalm 27:14 (KJV) - *"Wait on the LORD: be of good courage, and he shall strengthen thine heart: wait, I say, on the LORD."*

    We make the feeble attempt to wear what I call an "accessory of perfection" to bring attention to our own personal piety, instead of being the relatable person that people need to enact purposeful change in their lives. We spend endless amounts of time seeking out ways to paint pictures of perfection for others viewing pleasure and for our colleagues in ministry. We tend to run into disappointment because the perceptions that we have created are unrealistic. They are not sustainable and too tedious to maintain. As ministers of the gospel, it is easy for people to put you on a pedestal. These pedestals can be extremely high. They are so high that we often are overwhelmed and seek to take on a posture of seeking perfection to keep steady footing. If we fall, the likelihood of recovery is rare and we simply become "yesterday's news." Our time becomes consumed in the attempt to present a picture of "outward perfection," which is inward chaos and we place ourselves at the mercy of an unrealistic reality. The truth is that no one is perfect. People will not get it right all of the time. Yes, I am talking about everyone, even the man or woman of God. We have to understand that we must do the absolute best we can, maintain our integrity, walk in sincerity among the people and construct our character. God calls us continually into areas that demand both our time and attention. We put ourselves at a severe disadvantage when we simply focus on one simple facet. In order to be successful, we must learn to prioritize strategically to make things work in order. God is on our side to bless our efforts and he is always concerned. It is not how much you can do, but rather it is about how much you can do effectively with results that follow. Many of the clergy, both male and female, find themselves busy and booked. However, they are going nowhere. The majority of church leaders struggle with imbalance and instability. When imbalance occurs, women and men of God seem to fall through the cracks with no accountability. We live in a generation of spectators that will watch you fall, snicker, mock your injured state and wait to see if you will actually die. It is important that the mental state of the leader remain healthy as well as their physical state of wellness.

The practical sentiment is that with this nature of imbalance comes the inability to manage the places of their own anxieties. Due to this nature, the ministers and ministry leadership tend to develop a sense of loose transparency or oversharing. Due to the current state of culture, this overexposure within the church world is hailed as authenticity. On the other hand, it becomes the exposure of vulnerabilities that can lead to places of public attack. The congregation becomes the innocent bystander to which all of the emotions are released and dumped on them. Though these instances can occur outright, they can be done subliminally as well. Either way, these types of circumstances can be destructive on a grand scale. We have to learn to appropriately self-regulate and manage the places of our own anxiety. When we negate the management of these issues, we neglect our responsibilities as leaders. It can be noted that leaders that often come across as 'authentic,' in reality, may actually be lacking interpersonal and emotional boundaries. When a leader in ministry does not set forth an example of these interpersonal boundaries, they distort and set a misaligned standard of what authenticity should actually look like within the faith community.

It is unfortunate that we live in a society and church world that praises the public image, but neglects the necessity of building the whole person in private. Therefore, we are a public success but a private failure. We have become superficial and sensational. We have become afraid of exposure. We put on strength, gifting and talent as if they are decorations. We mask the person that we really are and continue to pay the overwhelming price on every level. Eventually, it becomes too much to bear and leads to a breakdown. There is a lingering fear of exposure. We are very afraid that people will discover that we miss the mark, we make mistakes and that we are human. It is the looming pretense surrounded by this feeling of the unveiling our vulnerabilities that pushes us to hide the places of our fragility that need to be addressed and prevent us from being genuine. When we are not in a place of sincere authenticity, we fail to deal with the "person" that we are and graft ourselves to the public personality that we want everyone else to see. The ever-present truth that confronts each of us, as ministers of the gospel, is that there are times in our lives when we will be directly confronted with hurt. We will face places of distress head on and will not be able to escape. This environment is not the most ideal.

Our strengths are visible and we lean towards revealing those at every angle. We love for our abilities to be acknowledged. All of the great things about ourselves we do not mind people bringing those to light. However, when it comes to our weak places or deficits, we do not want those revealed because they present us as being weak. We do not want our insecurities to left out in the open for the entire world to critique. We do not want to feel or be viewed as insufficient in the roles that we stand in on a daily basis as leaders. We must remember, even as ministry leaders, we are not exempt. We are 100% percent human and there is nothing wrong with that at all. Guess what that means? We are not perfect. The question we are forced to confront is why do we continue to fantasize or put on a sham? Why do we put on phony faces? Why do we hide behind counterfeit identities?

The reason we do this is the fear of rejection. One of the greatest struggles that clergy suffer with is rejection. Rejection can push us to the breaking point. The word rejection strikes fear and even resentment in the greatest of us. We have all experienced rejection in some form or fashion. We are afraid for people to see us as we are because we are fearful that they will frown on us or not hold us in high regard. In the age of social media and various Internet platforms, there are many who gauge their success by the parameters of people they do not even know. If they do not receive the likes or the hearts, they feel as if they are not relevant and then attempt to add things to themselves that would make them appear to be more attractive to the natural eye. Everyone has the desire to be included and wanted. No one wants to be avoided or cast aside. In truth, all of us desire to be supported, validated and loved. God loves us and that is critical to note. With God's love, comes his affirmation. However, there is a yearning to be acknowledged by the people that matter to us the most and our surrounding community. When we feel as if we are unloved or unnoticed, it can push us to pick up some dangerous additions that may not be to our benefit. The solution to the problem regarding the fear of rejection is to remain confident in God's love for us. The Bible says in Galatians 1:10 (KJV) – *"For do I now persuade men, or God? Or do I seek to please men? For if I yet pleased men, I should not be the servant of Christ."* We, as ministers of this great gospel, cannot afford to structure the ideals of our self-value around people that love us on a conditional basis. In doing so, we will only become disappointed.

Too often, as ministers and leaders, we spend too much time trying to gain the attention and acceptance of people who really do not matter. We seek the affirmation and validation of every person except the one who called us, which is God. We live life by design choosing our style, preferences and all these other things. We focus on fueling a perception, which is fragile and cost too much to maintain. We cannot afford to take up residence in the place of man's opinion, especially when we are "the called" of God. We are to fully rely on God to keep us from breaking and succumbing to the pressure of creating false identities. The Bible says in Jude 24-25 (KJV) – *"Now unto him that is able to keep you from falling, and to present you faultless before the presence of his glory with exceeding joy, to the only wise God our Saviour, be glory and majesty, dominion and power, both now and ever. Amen."*

"We are dismantled by the things we refuse to deal with!"

-Dr. Robert O'Keefe Hassell

When we neglect ourselves, we enter into a cycle called "dismantling." Everything around us seems to unravel because the reality is that in spite of what people interpret as us being okay we are actually crumbling from the inside out. However, there comes a time that the reality of our own humanity confronts us. It handles us in such a sobering manner. Often times, it is weighty and heavier than we could ever imagine. The reality within our current society does not address the humanity of the vessel. Pastors and ministers are human. Period.

We fail to address our needs as people because we take on the attributes of maintaining a personality within platforms strictly confined to a certain role or position. Our world outside of church could be spiraling and on the brink of destruction. However, if we choose to maintain the illusion that everything is okay, no one will question or think any differently about us. In the present day, many clergy have become comfortable operating in the dysfunctional. It has become commonplace for us operate from depleted places. As a result, this is a recipe for disaster and can destroy the very people we are trying to build if we are not careful.

The true struggle for many clergy is that they lack boundaries and balance. It is evident that Pastoral duties are becoming more extensive and challenging as the church takes on many endeavors that take on radical, non-traditional forms. Pastors and ministerial leadership find themselves overwhelmed. Leaders are operating at capacity in regards to handling multiplicities of issues among the people. These issues not only carry physical ramifications, but also present a series of emotional realities that need to be processed in healthy spaces. Our call by God commissions us to do extensive work for the sake of the Kingdom of God. However, there are necessary places that must be confronted in regards to-handling our humanity after the anointing lifts. Too many of us find ourselves, broken, discouraged, hopeless, suicidal, delusional and in denial. We take on things, more often than we should, as an outlet to avoid dealing with the critical problematic places that are preventing our forward moment. We have to understand that it is okay to "be weak." Every task we undertake will not be easy. More often than not, things will not go according to plan. However, when we are in relationship with God combined with spiritual alignment and natural balance, we can actually live. We can only be effective in our pastoral and ministerial leadership capacities when we become our first advocate in being "whole."

Confession is one of the most powerful, yet pivotal exchanges we can have with God. Being that he is all-knowing, he knows the depths of our hearts, our desires, our strengths, our weaknesses and most of all our final destination. He does not interrogate us, yet he gives us the opportunity to approach him freely and dialogue with him as a loving father. As leaders, in any capacity, it can be so easy to forget that we are human. We become so preoccupied with perception that we focus on maintaining image instead of maintaining right-standing in our relationship to our main source of accountability, which is God. In ministry, there are so many situations that happen to us and some instances where we may inflict hurt upon other people intentionally or unintentionally. There unresolved issues that we harbor in our heart, replay and re-run in our psyche, and attempt to bury in the dirt of our souls hoping that it will never rise again. However, the fact that we do not confess those things allows our lives to become toxic and the spillover to become harmful to others connected to us!

Confession is a form of confrontation. It hurts! We have to be truthful in our dealings with God and ourselves. Confession, although confrontational in nature, is necessary! The reason it does so is because it exposes our shortcomings, places of denial and puts us in a place of openness. The power behind confession is that when we confess to God, it puts us in a place and presence of the one who can touch us intimately and relieve us of the burden of all things that are hidden from the natural sight of other people. There is no greater feeling when you "come clean" and lay it all on the table with God. He fixes, restores, resets, and renews you in ways you could not even imagine. Remember, Proverbs 16:1-3 (KJV) - *"The preparations of the heart in man, and the answer of the tongue, is from the LORD. All the ways of a man are clean in his own eyes; but the LORD weigheth the spirits. Commit thy works unto the LORD, and thy thoughts shall be established."* Confess to God. Come clean, so you can be clean!

There are places in our life and ministry that we may be weak, but we do not have to break. The Bible says in Romans 15:1 (KJV) – *"We then that are strong ought to bear the infirmities of the weak, and not to please ourselves."* It is important that we assist each other, remain accountable and encourage each other. If professional help is needed, go out and seek it to maintain steady footing. Your influence and impact depends on you being in a healthy place. Yes, life may cause you to bend. However, you will not break! As the word says in Ephesians 6:10 (KJV) – *"Finally, my brethren, be strong in the Lord, and in the power of his might."*

Chapter 4
"When Revelation Meets Reality."

"Revelation is DIVINE DISCLOSURE by God on what to DO. Reality is the CONTEXT in which you PRODUCE and PERFECT what has been DISCLOSED."

-Dr. Robert O'Keefe Hassell

Revelation is preternatural means of interaction from God to man. God gives this measure of this sacred disclosure either orally or by writing in a printed form. In truth, revelation is found within the whole contents of what we know as the Holy Bible, which is the written Word of God. Through revelation, God takes the time to unveil himself completely in his entirety. He communicates several things to us as he unveils himself. We are able to see his ethical resolve and his justifiable efforts concentrated towards redemption through the sending of Jesus the Christ. As clergy and believers, we must fully understand that revelation is possible. God uses revelation for the purpose of always reaching his expected end. He affords us the full opportunity to engage him by realizing the conceptual understanding of the material evidences of God through salvation and the practical measures that align with our natural walk in this life.

It is through revelation that we come to know the clarity of our function in missive, ministry and purpose. In our human nature, we have the propensity to be narrow-minded and only see what is in front of us. Thus, it makes us 1-dimensional in our approaches that lead to "plateaus" in our methods and lead to frustrations in ministry. This state of narrow mindedness often makes recognizing purpose and subsequent function in our ministry roles rather difficult. Divine revelation can remedy man's natural deficiencies within reality. It bridges the gap between God and us. As practicing ministry leaders, whose roles are ever evolving, we must understand that this measure of revelation carries accountability and obedience to authority. As the vessels that God makes choice of using for his sacred service, we must understand as men that this revelation is inclusive of the absolute mandate for creed and conduct, for faith and practice: as he has indicated it within the scriptures.

Revelation is the source of the methodology or knowledge that is necessary to assist in our mandate to reconcile, reconnect and reestablish the people to their God.

We must consider that revelation does not coexist with reality and fact. There is yet a realm of the unknown, which God has not disclosed to men. Even while functioning in what he has revealed, there is a lingering expectancy of further revelations. We eagerly await a diverse series of divine releases. Revelation carries a responsibility and trust in the one who holds it in his possession. To possess the revelation of God, it must satiate the intelligence, reposition the predilections, hasten the longings, encourage the morality, and shape the integrity. God dispenses Revelation for the sake of our practical use. It is given to us to do all that he has purposed according to agenda as stated in Matthew 6:10 (KJV) – *"Thy kingdom come. Thy will be done in earth, as it is in heaven."* In giving us this revelation, God enters into a period of transactions with us as with perceptive individuals, proficient of accepting his will, qualified of executing him well-organized service. There is no ignorance in any of God's gifts. As soon as we have increased to the extreme our realization of God's will, we shall receive beyond. Psalm 25:14 (KJV) states, *"The secret of the LORD is with them that fear him; and he will shew them his covenant."* Since this is the case, we will come to "know" if we intentionally follow the Lord. Authentic submission amplifies the dimensions of knowledge; it increases the passion for greater spiritual attainment; it initiates hope.

Apostles, prophets, evangelists, pastors (or "shepherds") and teachers, remain active and valid offices in the contemporary Christian church of today. These five – fold ministry gifts have been assigned to the body for the purpose of edification and continual alignment. These capacities are still very much active in the church of today! However, we have become "hyped and conditioned" to prefer the perceived glamour of a specific position. We often taint the sanctity of these roles by infusing them with a hierarchy rooted in ego, ulterior motive and agenda, false humility and control. These are unhealthy and come against the efforts for unity required within the body, but they are impeding the progress of the kingdom agenda. It is stifling the effectiveness of our role to change the world 1 soul at a time. We have to understand that revelation meets reality when we come to understand the basics of two principles and the difference between both of them. These two factors are called giftedness and anointing. Unless we are able to properly process and make a distinction between the two, we will render ourselves ineffective to the people that truly need our help the most. Yes, the world needs our gifts. However, we remain ineffective unless the anointing is accessed and infused with the gifts we have been given.

Gifted (*adj.*) – Having exceptional talent or natural ability. People are gifted when their ability is significantly above the norm for their age. Giftedness may manifest in one or more domains such as intellectual, creative, artistic, leadership or in a specific academic field such as language arts, mathematics or science.

It is important to note that all gifted people do not look or act alike. Giftedness exists in every demographic group and personality type. It is important that people look hard to discover potential and support gifted people as they reach towards their personal best.

Anointing (*v.*) - the ritual act of pouring oil over a person's head or entire body in token of their being set apart for religious service. As a rite of inauguration in the Jewish Commonwealth anointing was intentional and a measure of distinction. Anointing was used to identify the chosen in three classifications prophets, priests and kings (Flemming, 1998).

The truth is that 'giftedness' alone cannot sustain you. It is simply not enough. The anointing is the carrier of purpose! The anointing precedes the assignment. We can only lead effectively with influence when we have the anointing.

Too often, we rely on just the gift. When we rely on the gift and lack the anointing, we tend to deplete quickly and fall apart. When we become too comfortable and dependent on giftedness, it can lead to our extinction. We must understand that giftedness is ineffective without the presence and power of the anointing upon our lives. The Bible says in Isaiah 10:27 (KJV) – *"And it shall come to pass in that day, that his burden shall be taken away from off thy shoulder, and his yoke from off thy neck, and the yoke shall be destroyed because of the anointing."* We live in an age where giftedness seems to take precedence over the anointing. However, the anointing is accompanied by a series of tangible evidences that cannot be denied (Empereur, 1982). The anointing over our lives is so powerful. This is the reason the enemy seeks to attack it so intensely with everything possible. The enemy is no match for the anointing of God. However, his attack centers itself towards the vessel that carries it. There are three purposes in which the enemy seeks to come against the anointing that resides in God's chosen. His agenda is to do the following in sequence: Deter, Delay, and Distract. He comes to attack the anointing over our lives in literal 3-D.

When we are deterred, delayed and distracted we discard revelation. Ultimately, we throw away our assignment and forfeit the progress. We put the lives of people at risk when we are out of purpose. We do so by neglecting the practical application of revelation to our practice. We become part of the problem instead of the solution. Today's church and ministry leaders are drawn to the prominence of position and the public affinity for the platform. It easy to treat church like "show time" instead of the sacred task and opportunity that it really is. We have to be attentive to the fact that we must refrain from allowing our ministry service (from without and within) to be tainted by the hype and cliché's. We live in an age where we are dealing with a people that require authenticity in its truest form. When we buy into the identity of creating a pre-packaged presentation, we take away the intent of the experience and become a disservice to God. Our greatest mistake is making "our agenda" the priority of the day. Our agenda has no place in the face of our divine assignment.

The anointing of God carries the agenda for our assignment. It is the intention and endorsement of the action that will be performed under the influence of the Holy Ghost. Luke 4:18-19 (KJV) – *"The Spirit of the Lord is upon me, because he hath anointed me to preach the gospel to the poor; he hath sent me to heal the brokenhearted, to preach deliverance to the captives, and recovering of sight to the blind, to set at liberty them that are bruised, [19] To preach the acceptable year of the Lord."* The anointing is necessary for us to function effectively within our ministry capacities. As leaders of all different age demographics, it is critical that we seek for more than just the emotional responses of people. The goal of our ministry should influence transformative change within the lives of the believer and unbeliever. The anointing is the place where we develop our hunger to pursue God. A "good close" or "shout" is simply not going to cut it. We need the anointing of God! We must realize that the anointing is a gift from God to those people that he has selected from among many to carry His presence and power in a sustainable way that bears witness to himself (Shelton, 2000). We must not settle. We must seek for the full manifestation of the anointing on our lives as we serve our various ministries, leaders, and God's people. As pitchers poured out for the restoration of people, we must extend our faith and intentionally avail ourselves to receive the purpose contained within the anointing to enact what

God has chosen us to accomplish in the earth. Jesus was a chosen vessel ordained by God for the intentional work of salvation. Jesus issued the promise of the Holy Spirit upon ascension and ensured that we would carry a power that would make our work for the kingdom operative. In the present day, because of the appeal, people tend to seek out popularity over the anointing. Very few desire this level of anointing because it involves the supernatural and great sacrifice. Therefore, they substitute the anointing for a giftedness that can grow them a following, but not help anyone.

When a person is a carrier of the anointing, they carry with them the ability of God to perform great works. John 14:12 (KJV) says, *"Verily, verily, I say unto you, He that believeth on me, the works that I do shall he do also; and greater works than these shall he do; because I go unto my Father."* The anointing is a very visible attribute one specifically, that people are attracted to in many cases. People recognize the presence of God on us through the expressions and the works combined with evidence that follows. As ministry leaders of all classifications, we are carriers of the anointing only by God's grace and ordained by God as such. We should not error by idolizing men because of the anointing, but rather esteem the fact that they are able to carry the anointing by the grace of God alone. Furthermore, in this present day, we tend to play the compare and contrast game. We tend to seek God and petition him to give us something that we cannot sustain or endure the process to get. Instead, we imitate them in our ministries. God does not deal in the area of duplication. God has designed a specific anointing for each one of us that carries intentional measures distinctive power and influence.

If you want to cultivate the anointing in your life, you must identify and submit to the one who anoints. Secondly, we must seek God in a way that He will divulge the plans He has for your life. Thirdly, we must relinquish our plans and unselfishly follow Him. Not everyone can do this because of the many personal reasons that they choose to bring up to negate the call on their lives. Many choose to walk away from the call because they refuse to follow or submit. The anointing becomes accessible through submission and requires taking an active approach in pursuing it.

As ministry leaders, we must develop a sincere hunger and thirst that will bring the anointing to us. There is an instance where God chooses whom he anoints, but there is a side to this where a person can seek God and obtain it. The same procedure is in place for seeking anything from

God that we desperately need. Matthew 7:7-8 (KJV) – *"Ask, and it shall be given you; seek, and ye shall find; knock, and it shall be opened unto you: For every one that asketh receiveth; and he that seeketh findeth; and to him that knocketh it shall be opened."* We access the anointing by faith. Our faith, once ignited, begins the journey of an active walk in assurance. Thus, the opportunity for the anointing presents itself to work fully within us.

Chapter 5

"From Grace to Growth!"

"When you authentically WEAR your GRACE, you move from GIFTEDNESS to GREATNESS."

-Dr. Robert O'Keefe Hassell

In ministry, authenticity is so paramount. Currently, we have too many people in ministry striving to be the best version of someone else rather than the first-rate version of themselves. When God called me, I knew what he called me to do along with the gifts he had given me. I was not in denial. I was disobedient and I ran. I was already awkward and I did not want anything additional that would make me "weirder" than I perceived myself to be already. As I began in ministry, I genuinely felt like I had my whole life, which was a late bloomer. To be candid about it, I felt like the kid in school who planted his grass seed in the milk carton and it did not grow while all of the other kids' seeds grew. After a while, the teacher moves the carton without you even noticing. Then boom, all of a sudden, you have the tallest grass in the class. My two take-aways were the following lessons:

1) Just because your PROGRESS appears to be UNNOTICEABLE to anyone else, does not NEGATE the fact that you are GROWING.
2) A LATE BLOOMER is NEVER LATE. It simply has an APPOINTED TIME!

We live in an age of duplication where we are attracted to what "appears" to be advancing. We cannot be persuaded by simple appearances. Looks can definitely be deceiving. Similarly, ministry can be the same way. You can have the platform, but lack the proper perspective to maintain it as a visionary. You can have influence, but lack integrity. You can have charisma, but lack character. In the present day, we must be cautious in exhibiting pseudo-'authenticity' that is being practiced popularly in the Body of Christ today. We have to remain true to our responsibility, our assignment, our intentions and ourselves. The critical priority is that our character and integrity align to create a core of consistency within who we are. We cannot allow this pseudo-authenticity to creep in and indirectly place the responsibility on the people around us for outcomes. We must take full responsibility for our actions and who we are.

Awareness is a critical aspect that we often miss when it comes to ourselves within context of the ministry. Awareness helps us understand who we are, what we are made of, how we are positioned in conjunction with other people, the appropriate nature of relationships, boundaries and the balance to sustain it all. First, awareness is paramount to understanding how "you" work. In ministry, no matter the capacity, self-awareness is the key to assisting you in the oversight of managing both your emotions and behavior. The ability to manage ourselves in a variety of scenarios inside and outside of ministry dynamics determines who we are when it comes to proactively connecting to those within and without. It is through this measure of conscious self-regulation that we are able to enact appropriate reactions and responses. We become capable of handling things with a conscious mind and with a solution-oriented approach. We maintain a consistently proactive posture by seeking ways to advance, re-connect and re-establish.

Awareness, self-awareness, is the catalyst for fueling our authenticity within any given context within ministry. It is important that we take the time to reinforce self-knowledge and put introspection into practice. It gives us appropriate insight to the areas in our lives and ministry where we need to strengthen ourselves, grow, expand our scope and reach beyond our self-imposed limitations. In ministry, we have to go in the environment knowing "who" we are. If you lack awareness of "who" you are, it is easy to misinterpret who you are becoming and distance yourself from your purpose. When you find yourself out of detached from purpose, the people that you are shepherding or leading are at risk. Your identity is discovered at the root of your self-awareness.

Many pastors, ministers and ministry leaders make the mistake of trying to design their identity around the simple tenets of their own perception of other personalities that are deemed to have the "it" factor. They adapt or make feeble attempts to mimic traits and styles, which hinder the authenticity of the ministry they have actually been given. Even though they may have limited success in exhibiting these types of behaviors, it is often short lived. They arrive at a place of crisis realizing that they are not only unfulfilled, but they are out of the will of God and have missed opportunities to cultivate the power of authenticity in their own anointing. Do not waste any more time! Quit attempting to become what God has not created you to be. If you do, you will be highly unsuccessful in the endeavor. Instead, make the choice to prove God right by walking the path and embracing it the way he intended specifically for you. I want to encourage those of you who are struggling and playing the compare/contrast game to stop today! You have nothing to prove! You are not competing against anyone! The kingdom is need of who you are and not who you perceive yourself to be. In this critical time in our world, God is not only calling us not to walk in grace, but also wear the grace we have been given.

Grace *(noun or verb)* - Unmerited divine assistance given to humans for their regeneration or sanctification; A virtue coming from God; A state of sanctification enjoyed through divine assistance.

God has given us each a specific grace for the assignment that he has called us to perform. Despite the level or depth, do not make the mistake of discounting it. Do not neglect what God has endowed, but rather embrace it within its fullness. With grace that he gives us, there comes both protections and provisions coupled with insight. Joseph, the dreamer, was "graced" to be the provisionary outlet for his family and all of Egypt during famine. He possessed the intellect, insight and innovation to make the most of the resources that were given to him to save the lives of many.

Of course, in his development, he faced ridicule and rejection. However, he understood that development was necessary to reach destiny. No matter what he was faced with, he wore his grace. When betrayed by his brothers and thrown into a cistern, he wore a protective grace. Sold into slavery in Egypt and into Potiphar's house only to be mishandled by his wife, he carried a responsible grace coupled with integrity. Thrown into prison, he was not only protected once again by his grace but he was given proper placement amid the cupbearer and baker. Had he never been thrown in jail, he would have never met the cupbearer. Thus, his gift of dream interpretation – an "operative grace" never would have been able to be revealed. If his operative grace had not been revealed at the appropriate time, all of Egypt and the surrounding lands would have perished. All of this being said, people in this world are waiting for you to wear your grace authentically without fail. The conditions of their souls, lives and livelihoods depend on it. You cannot afford to play pretender or attempt to be someone else. You have to be who you have been designed to be. We are assigned to a generation that needs to know grace, but made aware of its accountability. Our generation needs to become acquainted with mercy, but be made aware of its unwavering and unconditional follow-through.

The paradox of this present age is that, as ministry leaders, there is an intense urge to be "liked" instead of "respected." In all truthfulness, we can all attest that being "liked" and being "respected" are two different things. Due to the fact of our desire to be liked by everyone, we will attach and create identity modifications in order to appease people. As a result, we become our own delay by remaining disillusioned by our distractions. These push us further away from our path to destiny. We miss our intended purpose in the pursuit of gaining a platform or become a popular personality. We must remember that our call from God comes with a subsequent mandate. We have no choice but to fully embrace the will of God for our lives. We must authentically embrace it with everything inside of us! We must be careful not to "bleed" on the people. We must demonstrate our authenticity in such a way that the quality of our exposure in of brokenness points to the direct adornment that comes in God's grace. An authentic person is one who is not just keeping up outward appearances to satisfy perception, but completely walking out the journey of renewal through sanctification. However, no matter the process, the glory of God is yet revealed in their lives.

As you go forward in ministry and leadership, remember your authenticity will be your greatest asset. We should make no mistake in thinking that our identity is something that we can just graft, conjure or attach to ourselves. In doing things such as this, we can make a "monster" of our personal identities and ministries. We have to let our authenticity pour from the inside out. We understand that leadership is a process that deals with our emotional dispositions. Our skills and training are great, but there is nothing more powerful than looking within to discover what God is developing in us. What he is molding inside of us is not just for the now, but it is for the greater that lies ahead in the days to come. Looking within is one of the hardest task that God will ever ask you to do, but it is both necessary and worth it. It is the requirement. The place of self-examination that God calls us to is the standard that test our own sincerity and willingness to change. An individual's ability to be authentic gauges the sincerity and intentionality of the work that the leader puts in on a regular basis to develop themselves for a greater cause. When a leader lacks the ability to be authentic and fails to differentiate between the various dimensions of-his person, he becomes vulnerable to perception as well as opinion. Leaders can fall prey to the approval, acceptance, and affirmation of people because they become dependent on these factors for validation of places of current success. It is only when leaders can stand before others, not needing their affirmation, acceptance, and approval, that they are then truly free to be 'authentic.' When 'authenticity' is sought out based on one's need for approval, then leaders end up violating healthy interpersonal boundaries and bleed all over the congregation.

1 Corinthians 2:11 King James Version (KJV) says, *"For what man knoweth the things of a man, save the spirit of man which is in him? Even so the things of God knoweth no man, but the Spirit of God."* There is not another person in existence that "knows you" like you do! Even what you know about yourself is limited and even flawed in perspective. However, there is one greater that knows everything about who you "are" and what you are "not." If we seek to grow the people to whom we are responsible for being the role of under-shepherd, we must seek to establish a strong and balanced connection that is rooted in relationship. The reality is that our relationship must allow us to understand the nature of life's journey. We must be a visible representation as we walk with them and among them. We can leave an imprint on the people we lead from afar, but we can only provide inspiration to people who are in an adjacent position to us. When we are not afraid of articulating our failures and mistakes, we provide lessons to

people who are trying to find hope in the places that may be dark in their lives.

The ultimate goal of all spiritual leadership is that all people might come to glorify God. By seeing a tangible example though us of what his work looks like, they can come to understand and embrace true character of God as one who actively sustains. Ministry leaders across the country are challenged with the task of how to lead effectively, authentically and leave a Christ-centered impact on people that will lead to transformation. As leaders, when we wear our grace, the litmus test of its strength will be our character. Our character will determine our effectiveness as we strive to reach people. Character extends itself far more than ability does. People are seeking an authentic encounter with God. Essentials such as truthfulness, transparency, genuineness and a deep sense of purpose carry no financial expense. They are tangible things that remain accessible to everyone. At the end of the day, relationships are what count. The people that you are leading are in need of your time, your heart, your responsiveness and a chance to actually bond with other people. Our responsibility, with the help of God is to develop churches that elevate and extend community of faith. We are to lead in efforts to prioritize chances to serve, connect and grow together. We are the change we have been seeking and looking for all this time.

I would have never imagined becoming the man, minister and church leader I am today. Frankly, it was the furthest thing from my agenda. However, I could not imagine my life any other way. Despite the twist and turns, I am glad said yes and allowed God to guide me to this place in my life. My journey to this present place in ministry has been filled with adversity on many fronts. There were days that consumed themselves with unarticulated struggles. There were times where I was "looked over," has my "giftedness" used to almost the point of depletion, there were many questions that went without answers and moments of triumph. I can truly say that I have reached a point where I am able to embrace the fullness of "who I am in God" and embrace my call with accountability as well as maturity. I recognize my weaknesses and use them as fertilizer to grow them into strengths. God creates the grand script of our lives and equips us with everything we need to "BE." Some of you might not see the road in ministry that you are traveling as relevant or worthwhile, but you will arrive where you are intended to be under God's providence. We are gifts to the people that are connected to us and our world! Someone is waiting on you to "BE" what God purposed and ordained.

Life is one of the greatest gifts we have! It is an invaluable gift of time filled with moments of divine opportunity to become great and impact the lives of all we encounter. We only get one chance and must make it a priority to live it out with a sincere intent to become all that we can. God is consistent, unchanging and yet he moves with such awesomeness through the fiber and fabric of our very lives. He has predestined each of us to fulfill a God-given purpose while on this earth. He has called us to do "great works," especially in the days that we live in at present. John 14:12 (KJV) says, *"Verily, verily, I say unto you, He that believeth on me, the works that I do shall he do also; and greater works than these shall he do; because I go unto my Father."* In order for us to be effective and walk in the fullness of our purpose, we must endure a continual process through which God has orchestrated a series of experiences. The experiences will push us, grow us and change us to what he desires us to be!

As I reflect upon my own journey, I can say that it is evident that God is moving many of us to different places in him. For every level of growth, we come to understand the power and promise of the new grace that we receive. The dynamic of our social circles continue to change. There are times where we may even feel isolated and invisible. It is during these times that God begins to talk us through situations, heighten our discernment, purify our motives, give us guidance and correct us! At this very moment, in your life, the very hands of God are on you. They are re-molding, shaping, and building new things into your being. The process of it all will be uncomfortable, but it is beneficial to the development of our destiny. Many of us are at the doorway of destiny prepared to walk through it at any moment. However, there are just a few more things that God wants to do inside of us and we have to be okay with his processes to accomplish the result. There are times when God's methods of getting us to a certain place boggle us. Then again, in retrospect, they become clearer because we have to learn to become a master of the simple before we can take on the complex. For those of you that feel the ground shifting and scenery changing, be confident that you are closer to something mind-blowing that God has prepared. The promised place of destiny is not going to be like any place you ever experienced before. Therefore, the preparation is not going to be like anything you have ever experienced before. Trust the purpose behind the process and watch God do something amazing!

REFERENCES

Bible, H. (2000). King James Version. *Texas: National Publishing Company.*

Empereur, J. L. (1982). *Prophetic Anointing: God's Call to the Sick, the Elderly, and the Dying.* Michael Glazier.

Fleming, D. (1998). The Biblical Tradition of Anointing Priests. *Journal of Biblical Literature, 117*(3), 401-414.

Shelton, J. B. (2000). *Mighty in Word and Deed: The Role of the Holy Spirit in Luke-Acts.* Wipf and Stock Publishers.

Vitello, Paul (2010). *Evidence Grows of Problem of Clergy Burnout* - The New York Times

https://www.nytimes.com/2010/08/02/nyregion/02burnout.htm

ABOUT THE AUTHOR

Dr. Robert O'Keefe Hassell is a native of Lebanon, Tennessee. He attended Lane College in Jackson, Tennessee where he graduated in 2007, Summa Cum Laude, with a B.A. in English. In May of 2009, he graduated from Tennessee State University with his Master's in Education (M.Ed.) in Curriculum and Instruction with a concentration in Education Technology. In July of 2016, he completed his Doctorate of Education (Ed.D.) in Curriculum and Instruction with a concentration in Curriculum Planning within the Department of Teaching and Learning at Tennessee State University. Dr. Hassell has maintained a highly successful career in education since 2009. Currently, he works as Learning Support Staff-Writing at Tennessee State University. Additionally, he is an Adjunct Professor of English and the Writing Center Coordinator at American Baptist College.

He was licensed to preach the gospel on November 24, 2013 at the Trinity Missionary Baptist Church under the leadership of Reverend Earl Dirkson. On December 9, 2017, he was ordained as an Elder in the Churches of God In Christ, Inc. (COGIC) - Tennessee Eastern 2nd Jurisdiction by Bishop James M. Scott.

Currently, he serves as the Assistant Pastor of the Kingdom Love Worship Center (KLWC) in Madison, Tennessee under the leadership of Supervisor – Pastor San Franklin. Dr. Hassell serves as the National Dean of Christian Education for the National Preachers and Minister's Alliance (NPMA) based in Cleveland, OH. His civic, organizational and community appointments are as follows: Vice-President of the Hall-Davis-Alexander Scholarship Initiative (Lebanon, TN), a member of the Lambda Mu Sigma Chapter of Phi Beta Sigma Fraternity, Inc. (Murfreesboro, TN), a Life Loyal member of Phi Mu Alpha Sinfonia - Eta Xi Chapter at Tennessee State

THE CLERGY CONVERSATIONS

University, a member of P.B. Pegues Lodge #358 - Prince-Hall Affiliated Masons (Jackson, TN), and Sigma Tau Delta - Honor Society (English, Arts, and Humanities). He credits his development to God, the act of community investment, and the unwavering support of his family for his successes.

www.ingramcontent.com/pod-product-compliance
Lightning Source LLC
Chambersburg PA
CBHW071226160426
43196CB00012B/2426